FAMILY BUSINESS LEGACY PLAN

THE ULTIMATE GUIDE TO CREATING A LEGACY FOR YOUR FAMILY WITHOUT PAYING TOO MUCH IN TAXES

MARIA L. ELLIS, MBA

"Maria captures both the mind and the heart of the *Family Business Legacy Plan* process and does so in a fluid and accessible manner. Her poignant examples and stories lend further credence to the practical tips and tools that are relevant across cultures. She effortlessly captures the unique, and sometimes difficult to articulate, aspects of a family dynamic as distinct from other succession planning efforts. *Family Business Legacy Plan* is a must-read for all who are first or multiple generation family business owners grappling with this extremely complex process."

— JAYANT DAVAR, CO-CHAIRMAN AND MANAGING DIRECTOR, SANDHAR TECHNOLOGIES LIMITED

"If you are the owner of a family business and have not yet engaged in the process of creating a family business legacy plan, this book is a must-read. Maria masterfully takes you on a journey of discovery with relatable examples, informative data, and words of wisdom for the mind and soul. It is never too soon to create a plan that will give you confidence and peace, knowing your business succession is strategic, thoughtful, and harmoniously aligned with your family values."

— SARAH C. BAZEY, EXECUTIVE DIRECTOR, AMERICAN HIGHWAY

"I congratulate Maria Ellis on her new book that empowers business owners like myself with a blueprint to create and implement a fair and equitable legacy plan resulting in family harmony and peace of mind. With real life examples from her own challenges and diverse background, in her new book *Family Business Legacy Plan*, Maria carefully lays out the steps leading to a successful and financially effective family businesses succession. It should be a guidebook for many generations to come."

— FELEKŞAN ONAR, OWNER, FY-SHAN GLASS STUDIO

"I read Maria Ellis's book with curiosity. I was impressed by the specific knowledge of both the analytical and the human aspects of creating a family business legacy plan that is fair and equitable for all stakeholders. Maria's empathetic qualifies and ability to understand people makes her a unique family and business advisor. I highly recommend *Family Business Legacy Plan* especially for entrepreneurs who are focused on family and business legacy as a measure success."

— DR. ANTONIO SEGNA, BESTSELLING
AUTHOR AND BUSINESS ADVISOR

"Maria captures both the mind and the heart of the family business legacy plan process and does so in a fluid and accessible manner. Her poignant examples and stories lend further credence to the practical tips and tools that are relevant across cultures. She effortlessly captures the unique, and sometimes difficult to articulate, aspects of a family dynamic as distinct from other succession planning efforts. *Family Business Legacy Plan* is a must-read for all who are first or multiple-generation family business owners grappling with this extremely complex process."

"*Family Business Legacy Plan* is difficult and complex to face. The success of a well-planned and executed plan is one of the steps to guarantee the sustainability of the business as well as the peace and tranquility of the family in the years to come. Intelligence, knowledge combined with Maria Ellis' experience make *Family Legacy Business Plan* a must-read for everyone who has serious intentions in perpetuating what they have built professionally and personally."

— CHARLES S. ROTHSCHILD, CO-FOUNDER AND CHAIRMAN OF THE BOARD OF DIRECTORS, NAZAR SYSTEMS BRAZIL

"This is the business family legacy book that wealth managers should read to implement some of these legacy strategies to deepen their business relationship with their high-net-worth clients."

— PABLO M. CAIROLI, PRESIDENT, CAPITAL MARKETS ARGENTINA

"Maria has captured the essence of the family business legacy planning. She has communicated the soft and the hard factors to consider when thinking about creating a fair and equitable legacy plan. *Family Business Legacy Plan* is a must-read book for all family business owners across different cultures who would like to explore the succession planning process."

— DENNIS HU, DIRECTOR, AUSKIN AUSTRALIA

"Kudos to Maria for managing to provide, in a very readable format, so much valuable information as to how to avoid pitfalls when creating a family business or planning for the future of an existing family business as new generations take the helm. I found that her discussion of the impact of changes to estate and gift tax regulations on ownership planning for the business to be particularly important and enlightening, in light of the For the 95.5 Percent Act and other recent proposals being considered by Congress to overhaul current gift and estate tax exemptions."

— HELANE A. KIPNEES, ESQ., LASSER HOCHMAN, LLC

"Successful businesses thrive and succeed by making unemotional generally cost-effective decisions for the good of the enterprise. Bringing in family members or extended family members can create difficult challenges and opportunities for the founder and the success of the entity. It is not a coincidence that family businesses rarely succeed to the third generation. Maria Ellis's book does a great job of exploring these challenges and opportunities."

— RAY CICCOLO, OWNER, VILLAGE AUTOMOTIVE GROUP

"Picking up on Steven Covey's timeless advice to 'begin with the end in mind' and wise words from Harvard Classmate and family business leader Dan Sullivan, 'remember that happiness is a decision not a result,' Maria is aiming to help readers create the right state of mind for creating their family legacy plan. Filled with stories from family business leaders Maria has come to know, *Family Business Legacy Plan* acknowledges that success in family business sees inheritance not as a property right but a responsibility; we are keepers of the tangible wealth and the intangible goodwill created by their business. Whether you are the founder of a family business, or second, third, fourth or even tenth generation, you will find useful lessons and guideposts as you to work to preserve, maintain and grow the company until you pass the family business onto the next generation."

— CHRIS BRIDGES-TAYLOR,
EXECUTIVE CHARIMAN, BRIDGES
CAPITAL VENTURE PTY LTD, DIRECTOR,
BANDR ENCLOSURES PTY LTD

"Family Business Legacy Plan is a must-read for any family concerned with their legacy. Maria Ellis manages to explain in an intuitive and no-nonsense kind of way a step-by-step guide for the family to be confident about the path they chose and that it is in line with their values and their long term multi-generational objectives. For most families, *Family Business Legacy Plan* could be one of the best decisions they ever make."

— WENCES CASARES, CHAIRMAN, XAPO

"In *Family Business Legacy Plan,* Maria emphasizes the importance of nurturing business growth and family relationships synergistically. In a loving and empathic way, she invites us to consider how to create a fair and equitable family business legacy plan and I especially enjoyed reading how families across diverse cultures around the world manage legacy issues. *Family Business Legacy Plan* is a book that I highly recommend to families who want to start a family legacy plan but do not know how to start the process."

— JUAN FELIX ROSSETTI, OWNER, JFRF
NORTHSIDE LLC

"Maria's book encourages you to create and implement a family business plan that is in alignment with your family values to enable the next generation to grow socially responsible and continue to give back to the community. The right mindset and open communication are critical in creating a legacy plan that is fair and equitable for all stakeholders."

— FRANCISCO SURIANO , CEO AND COB, GRUPO FERROMAX

"Maria's analysis goes beyond simple succession planning. She has provided an ethos for capitalistic legacy planning and sustained generational wealth. She manages to divulge in detail the aspects of a family dynamic within business with ease. This is not simply a to do list, but a holistic strategic approach to maintaining both the financial and emotional support of one's family and business continuity. Highly recommend this read."

— LIN ROGERS, CHAIRMAN, ROGERS ELECTRIC

"Had my parents read and implemented the tools you outlined in *Family Business Legacy Plan* more than twenty-five years ago (prior to my father's unexpected passing at fifty-three years young), it would have made the transition from our first generation to second generation (my brothers and me) so much easier both professionally and personally. I hope and pray every business owner and entrepreneur utilizes your book to create their own unique family business legacy plan providing for business succession but also family peace and harmony."

— GEOFF TAYLOR, PRESIDENT AND
CEO, C3CONTROLS

CONTENTS

To our Harvard Business School OPM32 Enterprising Families around the world.

Maria Ellis has written the ultimate guide to creating a legacy. *Family Business Legacy Plan* is about a topic that is always important, generation after generation: how to ensure that a fair and equitable family legacy. Maria spent her entire career in the financial world, rising the ladder at a large and prestigious bank conducting international business and now in investment advisory including real estate. She deeply understands financial concepts and has given the gift of sharing her knowledge and expertise in a highly readable book. Maria captures both the mind and the heart of the Family Business Legacy Plan process and does so in a fluid and accessible manner. Her poignant examples and stories lend further credence to the practical tips and tools that are relevant across cultures. She effortlessly captures the unique, and sometimes difficult to articulate, aspects of a family dynamic as distinct from other succession planning efforts.

Maria's life story is inspiring. Immigrating to the United States with her family after graduating from high school in Guayaquil, Ecuador where she was born and spent her formative years, Maria pursued her BBA and MBA at the University of Massachusetts, and later enrolled in the Harvard Business School Owner-President Management program. This education allowed Maria to pursue her professional dreams and is a great example of the pillars in successful personal financial management which are: Saving; Investing and Estate Planning. Maria's analysis goes beyond simple succession planning. She has provided an ethos for capitalistic legacy planning and sustained generational wealth. She manages to share in detail the aspects of a family dynamic within business with ease. This is not simply a to do list, but a holistic strategic approach to maintaining both the financial and emotional support of one's family and business continuity.

Family Business Legacy Plan builds on the

foundational tools of Maria's bestselling book, *Achieve Financial Freedom*, a road map to financial success which serves as a helpful reference guide as you reach each of your personal and personal financial milestones. I should add that Maria possesses a great work ethic: she commits to doing her best in all that she takes on. In addition to her advisory services, Maria is a pro-bono consultant with the Harvard Business School Club of New York's Community Partners whose mission is to create constructive partnerships between Harvard Business School alumni and nonprofit organizations in the greater New York City metropolitan area that seek assistance with business and management issues.

Like Maria, I am a graduate of the Owner President Management Program, at Harvard Business School. I am an American-born actress, writer, television journalist and preservationist.

My late husband, HSH Prince Nicolò Boncompagni Ludovisi, was Prince of Piombino XII. His ancestors were placed in Spoleto, in 980, by Emperor Otto II, from whom he descends. Our home, Villa Aurora, is a designated Italian National Historic Monument and was chosen by Google Culture as an important cultural site. It was built on the famed Gardens of Sallust, dating back to ancient Roman times. In fact, Ludovisi Gardens, 86.9 acres in size, was the largest and most celebrated garden, inside the walls of Rome. Its destruction was lamented by Stendahl, who stated the most beautiful gardens, in the world, have been destroyed.

Indeed, Ludovisi Gardens was an essential part of the Grand Tour of Italy. Tchaikovsky, Hawthorne, Henry James, Goethe, Gogol, all made their way to Villa Aurora. As well as, Caravaggio, Guercino, Brill, Valesio, Domenichino, Pomerancho, and so many other notables. Bernini played cards with Cardinal Ludovico Ludovisi, his best friends, on many evenings, in our Aurora room. The genesis of opera began, in our Aurora room, when on February 2, 1601, Vittoria Archilei, the famed sopranist, sang acapella, for the second owner of the villa, Cardinal Francesco Del Monte. It was the first time anyone had heard a woman's voice by itself. Up until that time, women sang polyphonically to God. People began to cry when they heard her magnificent voice and her mentor, Cavaleri was in attendance and rushed home to write the first opera. We have the only ceiling painting ever done by Caravaggio. It is an oil on plaster painting created in 1597, by the young twenty-two-year-old artist.

Our home was selected by Google Arts and Culture, as an important cultural destination, along with the Taj Mahal. Rutgers University funded the digitization of our archive, dating back one thousand years, and Professor Corey Brennan, the Mellon Scholar became our curator. The public can now access our archive at https:// villaludovisi.org/, where you will see twenty-five letters from Marie Antoinette and many other unseen treasures.

As you can well imagine, family legacy is tremendously important to me, indeed critically important to me. I am related to George Washington, through my ancestor, Ann Ball, Mary Ball, George Washington's mother was her half-sister. My ancestors went to America, in 1623, having been given a swath of land by the King. James Madison is also my direct relative.

I have promoted new research on the history of the property, as well as the creation of the scholarly resource the Archivio Digitale Boncompagni Ludovisi.

If you want to know how to create a family business legacy plan and do not know where to start, or if you need more clarity for important legacy questions, as applied to your life, Maria's book will be an invaluable font of information for all your queries. She makes this complex journey simple, clear, and fun. I know her knowledge has assisted me in making the right decisions, which I hope will protect my husband's legacy and my Garlington legacy for centuries to come.

— HSH PRINCESS RITA BONCOMPAGNI
LUDOVISI

I NEED TO CREATE A FAMILY BUSINESS LEGACY PLAN TO AVOID PAYING TOO MUCH MONEY ON TAXES

"Fear is a natural part of growth."

— DAN SULLIVAN

Recently, I received a frantic call from Stephanie, an import-export business owner in Buenos Aires, Argentina. Stephanie was referred to me by one of my clients for whom I had helped create a family business legacy plan. Stephanie's challenge was about the continuity and profitability of her business because she was operating in a very difficult socio-economic environment. Additional challenges included high taxes and currency fluctuation.

Taxes in Argentina are extremely high, and navigating the system with multiple overlapping taxes creates a significant business challenge. Stephanie was also concerned that the Argentinian government had imposed strict currency controls on firms as the country spiraled toward an economic crisis, and she was lamenting that the Argentinian peso had lost a quarter of its value in a month which erodes profitability especially because, due to her import business, she has accounts payable denominated in U.S. dollars.

Stephanie is an introvert, and she relies on facts, data, and reports. Her primary concern was to maintain the company as profitable to enable herself and her family to live a certain lifestyle. Stephanie found herself in a difficult situation and she was stressed out, had a hard time sleeping, and could not find a reasonable solution to her business concerns which became personal when sales and profitability deteriorated after so many years of hard work on her business. Stephanie was unhappy, she had lost the desire to continue to work. Also, Stephanie's health had deteriorated due to her anxiety of not knowing how best to manage these business and life challenges.

To help Stephanie, I needed to understand her overall business. Over a period of four weeks, we talked about the financial situation of her import-export business, how profitable it was, and what kind of transitions she was considering. Was she considering selling her business? We worked on creating a three-to-five-year financial forecast to determine the potential value of the business. We also talked about the most important issues that were facing her business and created a family business succession plan that allowed the company to grow, diversify, and minimize taxes while identifying currency hedging strategies such as foreign exchange-forward contracts to better manage Argentina's currency fluctuation. A currency-forward contract is a foreign exchange tool that can be used to hedge against movements between two currencies. It is an agreement between two parties to complete a foreign exchange transaction at a future date with an exchange rate defined today.

You may empathize with Stephanie's story because you may be experiencing anxiety and frustration with your business challenges and you are not able to solve – or at least minimize – the negative effects on your business.

If you are facing difficult business and family transition issues, keep reading this book because my objective throughout this book is to share with you some ideas about how best to create a fair and equitable family business legacy plan that will provide you with financial freedom and, more importantly, peace of mind and serenity in your golden years.

You, like Stephanie, may be concerned about the continuity and profitability of your business and paying too much money in taxes. You too will have to answer three critical questions needing specific answers.

- Do you want the business to continue?
- Is it time to sell the business or will a succession plan be the better option?
- Who in the family is willing and able to assume responsibility to make the business grow in sales and profitability?

These are familiar and important questions that many family business owners experience. These are difficult decisions, but I have helped many business owners obtain clarity around these important questions. Lack of clarity happens far too often when creating a family business legacy plan, but once you, as the business owner, achieve clarity, then you can create a fair and equitable family business legacy plan taking into consideration tax-efficient business structures to maximize the benefits for the business owner, family, and stakeholders.

I started this chapter by letting you know that fear is part of growth and will end this chapter by emphasizing the need to create a family business legacy plan to avoid paying too much money in taxes.

2

HOW I CREATED A FAMILY BUSINESS LEGACY PLAN FOR A PROMINENT CLIENT

"Success is not final; failure is not fatal. It is the courage to continue that counts."

— WINSTON CHURCHILL

If you are reading this book, it is probably because you too are experiencing and can relate with the family business legacy issues and concerns that nearly all business owners experience when grappling with the need to create a family business legacy plan. Indeed, this occurred with a prominent client of mine based in New York City, co-owned by an entrepreneurial woman with a business degree from Columbia University as well as an MBA from Wharton, and her husband, who had a marketing degree from NYU and received his MBA from Carnegie Mellon. This enterprising couple had created a highly successful real estate business in 1996 which, after twelve years of hard work, was consistently recognized for its marketing innovation, operational ingenuity and sustainable business achievements through numerous industry and trade association awards. On numerous occasions their business was in various "top 100" lists of companies that matter most in the real estate industry.

This couple's company provides real estate services to high net worth individuals and works closely with a team of professionals such as investment advisors, accountants and attorneys to provide a variety of financial services to their clients. These financial services are designed to maintain a sustainable business model to make it easier to locate and procure high and ultra-high net worth individuals on a worldwide basis looking to diversify their investment portfolios. The company provides unique luxury properties on a sustainable basis with unmatched efficiency. However, the company has recently faced great industry pressure due to global economic downturns which in turn has caused my client's historically-successful business to falter somewhat, and therefore was no longer a leader in its industry.

When it comes to real estate, the competition in New York City is fierce. They operate on a business model of providing personalized recommendations (often using algorithmic AI applied to acquisition criteria), all with the goal of enabling investors to increase their overall return on equity.

Like most entrepreneurs, the founding couple had a stressful life, but they were blessed with two wonderful daughters – ages thirty-four and thirty-six. This successful couple was also responsible for the primary care of the husband's eighty-five-year-old father, who suffered from Parkinson's disease. Obviously, they were grateful for what they had been able to build together, but in moments of candor, they often expressed the feeling that they were missing out on some of life's pleasures, such as spending time with and enjoying their three young grandchildren. Additionally, this successful, entrepreneurial couple had additional financial obligations to their other stakeholders, including employees, investors, and suppliers, plus they were often worried about paying far too much money on taxes which of course diluted their net income.

One of this client's biggest challenges was to

motivate their employees to innovate and to be creative, to do whatever is necessary to enable their company's future success, to acquire new clients, and to grow both in sales and profitability. To solve these issues, with my assistance this client decided to increase its communication within its family and amongst its employees, in particular with respect to the latter, through formal weekly meetings. In addition, they created a comprehensive strategic business plan, wrote a detailed succession plan, and identified and implemented an advisory board having both family and non-family members. The advisory board met on a quarterly basis to monitor the progress of the company's growth and profitability.

After creating their strategic business plan, this client delegated the sales and customer satisfaction experience to their eldest daughter, who had been working with the company on a part-time basis for many years, and was then working full time. This client also continued to retain and incentivize key employees, and established contingency plans for various unplanned exit events such as unexpected life events. The above-referenced contingency plan included purchasing key man insurance and other relevant insurance policies to protect existing private investors and other key business partners, who collectively own approximately 15 percent of their company. The key man insurance is designed to protect the needs of their business – for example, buying out selected private investors in the event of the demise of one or both of the founding couple – and whole life insurance coverage provides death benefits for their family at large.

At my encouragement, the founding couple also created a transition plan as a direct result of our weekly meetings. As business owners they needed to be prepared to identify the next generation of company leaders, properly implement the plan for executive leadership, and communicate their long-term vision for the company to the next generation of leaders whether they turn out to be family members or non-family industry experts. The eldest daughter, a graduate of the Chicago Booth School of Business, was trained on important fiscal and financial matters – the heart of the business. The younger daughter, a Wharton graduate, was also a dedicated entrepreneur who experienced successes in the entrepreneurial environment and had been involved in successful mergers and acquisitions. She was not participating in the day-to-day operation of the real estate business due to her other prior entrepreneurial commitments, but we knew that she and her older sister were highly educated and were gaining business experience to continue the family business legacy, should both decide to do so. For the founding couple of this exciting client, it was extremely important to honestly consider their family's lifestyle choices, evaluate their desire to continue the business legacy, and evaluate their skillsets and experiences in order to determine who is best suited for each given role and to foster growth accordingly. It is also the founding couple's intention to lay out the creation of carefully written employment agreements and bonus and equity incentive plans to ensure future leaders remain with our company through a transition.

With my assistance, this important client has also identified key stakeholders for their real estate business and have created an advisory board with both family and non-family members. Life is uncertain – the only thing that is certain is change – so we worked on an appropriate buy/sell agreement as part of a transition plan to ensure retention of their majority equity ownership of the company and, in the alternative, have identified an agreed-upon methodology for valuation should they eventually sell a significant portion of their equity. Importantly, it should be noted that this client would likely not have been able to create the aforementioned transition plan alone, and that in addition to my involvement they have had the helpful guidance of various other trusted professionals, consisting of attorneys, accountants, and insurance consultants with experience in business and succession planning.

Often, my clients ask me, "When is it the right time to start thinking about succession planning and preparing our family business for transition?" There are many opinions on this matter; however, it has been my experience when working with entrepreneurs that they cannot easily conceive of transferring power and control of the company assets until it is almost too late. Business owners who do not plan for transition are often faced with the less-than-appealing option of selling their business for much less than its true value or, alternatively, shuttering the business with no return upon that event. However, those who plan carefully can realize the value of their life's work: either by selling their business or passing on their business to the next generation and happily see their business legacy continue. It is not easy for a business entrepreneur who has created and guided the company for many years to seriously commit to sharing responsibilities with the next generation, but it must be done to maximize the value of the business.

Succession planning includes working with trusted advisors, creating a timeline, training, identifying positions needing both internal and external successors, getting involved and commitments from key players. Now that I have shared with you how this valued client has worked together with me and other valuable advisors to create and implement a successful family business legacy plan, I know that you too will feel energized and motivated to create a family business plan that meets your overall life objectives.

3

YOU CAN CREATE A SUCCESSFUL FAMILY BUSINESS LEGACY PLAN

"Coming together is a beginning; keeping together is progress; working together is success"

— EDWARD EVERET HALE

The purpose of this chapter is for you to learn the process of creating a family business legacy plan and feel excited about it. Creating a plan is easy once you learn the principles; however, the most challenging part of this book is to help create your right state of mind.

When you are creating and implementing your family business legacy plan, visualize your future self and your whole life considering this plan. It becomes the context of your life. Changing the context changes the meaning and possibility. You simply want to get clear on what you want three to five years from now. What does your future self's life look like? What does your future self's environment look like? Who are the main people in your life? What is the overall experience you are having? What does your typical day look like? What is important to your future self? Where is your focus?

Once you have envisioned your family business legacy plan, share it with your family, advisors, and other stakeholders and become accountable for creating and successfully implementing your family business legacy plan. Hearing yourself say it will cause you to believe it more. Your thoughts should become words, words should become courageous actions, actions habits, and habits your personality and destiny. When you begin making powerful decisions in your life, you are then enabled to prioritize your life. You can determine what success looks like for your future self.

If you decide to create and implement a family business legacy plan, you can do it yourself or you can hire an advisor to help you create a solid family business legacy plan and a faster implementation. A well-designed family business legacy plan minimizes federal, state, and city taxes and enables you to keep more money for your family and for charitable organizations that are in alignment with your values. You do not need to have all your family business legacy issues figured out to start the process, but you need to identify and prioritize your personal and business assets. In my experience, the biggest mistake successful business owners make is not to seek professional advice.

I have found that successful family business legacy plans reflect on questions such as:

- Who is considered a family member?
- What is the family vision for its role in the community?
- What are the family's and the business's core values?

It is important to involve family members in planning discussions because just announcing your plan without family involvement is the surest way to create family discord. Also, discussing the plan helps the business owner to identify who in the family wants to be involved directly and who is focused elsewhere. It also might help some family members find new opportunities and interest in the business. Other things to consider would be the protocol that should govern family members' sales and purchase of shares. For example, a buy-sell agreement can specify which family members are eligible to own stock (such as bloodline descendants only) and can prohibit the sale of stock outside the family. It is critical to communicate with your estate planner to ensure there is no uncertainty or confusion about your intentions.

If you have a successful business with more than one owner, a buy-sell agreement provides a smooth transition and continuity of management and ownership to the remaining business owners. A buy-sell agreement also provides the following benefits: it creates an instant market for a business interest that may not otherwise be saleable. It establishes a fair market valuation for federal estate tax purposes that is binding on the IRS. The buy-sell agreement specifies the terms of payment and is easily funded with life insurance. It also provides the liquidity to the retiring owner or to his estate in the event of death and provides funds to decedent's estate to pay estate taxes and administrative costs. A buy-sell agreement guarantees a fair return for a departing owner or their heirs and provides peace of mind and security for the business – the business owner's and their families. A buy-sell agreement is a practical result of comprehensive business succession planning. It is a legally binding document that protects the interests of a company's owners and permits the business to continue efficiently in the event of the death, disability, or retirement of a business owner.

Also, the business owner must establish and communicate the principles that will guide the leadership succession process in identifying and developing new leaders who can replace leaders when they retire or leave the organization. A family business best practices is a process based on developing a plan that increases the availability of experienced and capable employees and family members who are prepared to assume leadership roles, and to what extent and according to what criteria should family members be involved in the business and how will their performance be evaluated on an ongoing basis.

Finally, other considerations when creating and implementing your family business legacy plan are how the family should be organized and governed to achieve its vision and promote its family values. For instance, one of the business owners I surveyed prior to writing this book has two daughters who are passionate about non-profit and charitable work and giving back to the local community and were grateful that the business was able to provide the funds to help with local, regional, and global community projects. Throughout my research for this book, it was evident that philanthropic or other joint activities often promote family cohesion and bonding.

Now, I will tell you what you will learn throughout this book. In Chapter 4, you will start by setting goals for success and thinking about how best to create a fair and equitable family business legacy plan with a clear vision and peace of mind. You will start by doing an inventory of all your personal and business assets and working with advisors who will help you with the important and emotional decisions that you will have to make in the process.

In Chapter 5, you will identify your trusted advisors and decide to have an open communication with family members to enable you to start allocating personal and business assets.

In Chapter 6, you will envision your success by identifying and prioritizing the business products and services based on profitability.

In Chapter 7, you will learn to identify the family business challenges and opportunities. Some of the family business challenges and opportunities may include your decision of whether to sell or not to sell your family business. By making these important decisions, you will make sure that you do not lose money due to irresponsible choices or due to lack of a family business legacy plan.

In Chapter 8, you will think through and consult with your advisors about the best way to structure the business ownership.

In Chapter 9, you will continue to create and implement a plan that is in alignment with your values.

In Chapter 10, you will see how family business owners create a family business legacy plan that is fair and equitable for all stakeholders. You will know in your heart that you have a fair and equitable plan, and you will make it work with the cooperation of your advisors and family members.

In Chapter 11, you will face and decide how best to deal with the challenges associated with the implementation of your newly created family business legacy plan.

And finally in Chapter 12, you will feel happy that you have been able to successfully create and implement a fair and equitable family business legacy plan.

I am confident that after reading this book, you too can create a family business legacy plan if you are committed to the outcome of a well-thought-out plan that is equitable and fair and that will enable you to live your life in a peaceful and enjoyable lifestyle surrounded by your loving family. Most business owners are concerned about business succession and often have no idea where to start. Based on my survey with business owners, one of the first things to do is to decide to do it, and then surround yourself with stakeholders and business advisors who have in mind the business and the family's financial wellbeing. I always encourage business owners to learn the process of creating a family business legacy plan to minimize taxes and stop worrying about losing money due to irresponsible choices.

4

SETTING GOALS FOR SUCCESS

"The word responsibility is interesting because if you take it apart, it's actually the ability to respond."

— DAN SULLIVAN

According to SCORE, the nation's largest network of volunteers, expert business mentors reported that only 30 percent of family-owned businesses survive from the first to the second generation and only 12 percent survive from the second to the third generation. Yet, 47 percent of owners expecting to retire in the next five years do not have a successor. In this chapter, we will create a family business legacy plan with a clear vision and peace of mind. To create a clear vision for the business planning and continued success of the company, the business owner must reflect on the past, look at the present, and visualize the future to create an inspiring vision for the company. This vision will be a road map for its management and employees to actively participate and execute the business succession plan. If you anticipate transferring your business privately to family members or employees or if you are considering a sale on the open market, it is best to start planning for the transition sooner rather than later. Ideally, the transition should be a gradual, multi-year process due to the complexity involved in most business transition plans. For example, if you think you may be ready to exit your business in the next three to five years, now is the time to start that process. While that timeframe surprises some business owners, taking a long-term approach allows for a well-thought-out transition. It takes a team of many individuals to create and achieve a shared vision, and it often starts by reviewing and analyzing key questions such as:

- Who are we?
- What have we accomplished?
- What markets do we serve and provide value to?

- What are the company's strengths?
- What other markets can be served?

Although you may have specific goals for business growth and profitability, planning for various outcomes can help you be prepared for any contingency.

Cash-flow planning is an important component of strategic business planning for businesses at any stage of the lifecycle. Your plan should consider more than just who will assume ownership after the transition; it also needs to address how ownership will be structured. Tax implications are one factor in determining the structure of a deal; however, considerations such as the long-term goals of the family, the time frame of the transfer, as well as the level of control and involvement you will maintain during and after the transfer should all be addressed as well.

Transitioning a business can result in different tax ramifications for the business and its shareholders depending on how the deal is structured. Considering the different scenarios and how they relate to your objectives will enable you to make informed decisions. Business owners may have done extensive estate planning, identifying how personal assets should be managed in the event of business owner incapacity or death; however, many business owners fail to include their business assets in their estate plans, which can lead to time-consuming and costly estate administration. Planning for the orderly succession of your business involves more than just a handoff of financial responsibility and rights; it is also an opportunity to identify and train a successor who can continue running your business in the same way you would. Knowing that plans are in place can give business owners peace of mind.

As business owners approach retirement, some founder-owners tend to scale down their involvement in the day-to-day operations, leading to operational and financial issues and reduced customer service satisfaction while others maximize the opportunity for the second generation by creating and implementing a family business legacy plan. It is important to pay attention to the operational changes associated with transitioning ownership from the founder to the second generation including formalizing equity stakes and internal processes, establishing a clear organizational structure, and improving customer service.

While the traditional view of a family business is that first-generation business founders are the entrepreneurial heroes, the second generation of a family business does not have to live in the shadow of the first generation. In their book, *Entrepreneurs in Every Generation*, Allan R. Cohen and Pramodita Sharma specify the conditions supporting entrepreneurial and innovative behavior. The second generation plays a pivotal role in professionalizing the business and building out new initiatives, building on the legacy of the first generation to develop a great family, not just a great business. Successful second-generation leaders tend to focus more than the first generation on gathering and aligning disparate family members to create a strong family pillar alongside a well-developed enterprise pillar. The second generation is therefore crucial to pivoting the family away from a single-minded focus on business development to a broader set of initiatives where family communication, governance, and cohesion are fostered. For example, John D. Rockefeller was a titan of the Gilded Age. But his only son, John D. Rockefeller Jr., had the unenviable tasks of managing the family fortune and rehabilitating the family name after his father's reputation was in tatters, as he was accused of being a ruthless monopolist. Rockefeller Jr. mentored his five sons and his daughter, enhanced his father's charitable legacy, hired talented advisors to professionalize the family's investments and philanthropy, and prepared the burgeoning third generation for social and philanthropic leadership. It is often in the second generation that family councils are first considered – or at least the beginnings of more information-sharing and decision-making among siblings. The need for family governance may have been only slightly understood by the wealth creator, leading to incomplete or misdirected succession planning. The main question that arises in the second generation is not how the family can create more wealth, but rather what is the purpose of the wealth?

While doing research for this book, I read a Harvard Business School case study about "The 1,000-Year Plan." This forty-generation family business legacy plan was created by two brothers – David, age sixty-two, and Sammy Lee, age fifty-five – the fourth generation of the Lee Kum Kee family business – a sauces and condiments group that was a household name in Hong Kong, mainland China, and other parts of Asia. Established in 1888 and headquartered in Hong Kong, it was the largest manufacturer of oyster sauce in the world. Having recently celebrated its 130-year anniversary, the family had expanded considerably into other businesses as well as philanthropy, weathering two major breakups in its earlier years.

"I've seen family feuds from my father's generation and the generation before which have turned rather nasty. We want to prevent that from happening again," Sammy said.

In 2002, a family council – which oversaw the family business, family investment, and the family office – was established, and a family constitution was drawn up with the aim of building stronger family bonds. Since their father had bought out their uncle to gain full ownership, he was like the first generation of the family business, and so the five fourth-generation siblings – Eddy, Elizabeth, David, Charlie, and Sammy – considered themselves like the second generation. As such, they now had an opportunity to come up with a family system that was sustainable, and factored in the need to adapt continuously to change and was backed by the values that the family stood for.

Sammy noticed a few years back that the interests between the family members who participated in the family business had diverged more markedly from those who did not, and the fifth generation's engagement in the business was waning. Troubled that these were seeds for disunity in the future, in

2018, Sammy had the idea to create a system for the family with the next 1,000 years in mind and it would be called the 1,000-Year Plan. The fourth generation would involve their children, the fifth generation (G5), in co-creating this new system. Even though 1,000 years sounded unusually lofty, it did not strike Jamie Lee (daughter of Sammy) and Kevin Lee (son of David) as surprising. In fact, it was in line with what they always knew about the family mission, which was to help people in the community thrive as human beings by being kind, loving, healthy, and happy, by having empathy and being good to each other.

"The 1,000-Year Plan was created with the belief that we will work best as a cohesive family vs. a single family member," Sammy explained. "1,000 years is like forty generations. No one is going to live for 1,000 years, so it helps everyone to take a helicopter view so there is a better chance of getting consensus." As for the family legacy, Sammy said, "Recently I've been thinking that we should play down our legacy to make room for other people to create their own legacies." They decided they needed two new vision statements, one for the business and one for the family. They could boil down their corporate culture to three core values: (i) Si Li Ji Ren,

(ii) Constant Entrepreneurship, and (iii) Autopilot Leadership. Si Li Ji Ren in Chinese means "considering the interest of all before taking any action." Constant entrepreneurship was reinforced by their investing principle – with any new initiative, you do not need 100 percent certainty about its success before taking the risk; 60-70 percent certainty was enough. The autopilot leadership model – based on the "invisible leadership" concept in the Chinese philosophy of Daoism combined with Western management theory – advocated employees work independently and towards the same goal, like a car or a plane in autopilot mode, without the need for a leader to have hands-on command. They therefore settled on a new vision statement for the business: "Guided by the principles of Si Li Ji Ren, constant entrepreneurship, and autopilot leadership, we strive to be the most trusted enterprise for a healthier and happier world beyond 1,000 years!" Sammy qualified, "We realize that values can change over time, so we are open to adding new values."

One of the first restructuring moves under the new plan was to form a separate owners council to oversee the business side and family investments, which would be independent of the family council to achieve what they called the "extreme balance" between the family and the business. They called this "Family, Family First" and "Business, Business First" which, according to Sammy, meant, "If you go into our family lunch, you feel like this family doesn't have a business. And when you go into our business, you feel like this business doesn't have a family."

David likened this "extreme balance" to a high-wire act: "Imagine you have the whole family, like thirty-three members standing on top of your shoulders, and you have to balance on a high wire with a stick and walk across the Grand Canyon. How do you do that?"

They wanted a system that could allow for changes, so they inserted a clause in the Constitution stipulating that the owners council could change the Constitution with a 75 percent majority. They also changed the constitution so that family members could no longer be managing the day-to-day operation of the business to prevent conflicts. They feared that allowing family members to join the business might leave less room for outside talent. However, it could also trigger disengagement from the family. They wanted to make room for the scenario that a capable future family member could have a chance of becoming the CEO. "Although we don't encourage it," said Sammy. And the owners council could, in that case, allow it with a 75 percent majority. Since not everyone would work in the family's core business, they wanted to create more opportunities for family members to get involved. They focused on developing more opportunities for owners to participate in governance activities (governing ownership) and running board training programs on governance.

"You could be a governing owner and be on the board or in the family foundation. Or you could be a doctor and come to the family assembly and family retreat once a year," Jamie said.

Now that they had determined a new vision statement for the business, Sammy and David hoped that this brainstorming session would help them come up with one for the family. And should they eventually combine the two vision statements to make one combined vision or keep them separate? This question was an analogy for the next 1,000 years of the Lee Family: how will they hold the family and the business together in balance? Was it the best way to last 1,000 years? How should they incorporate future generations, point to celebrating diversity and the individual as well as the collective, and create a system that reinforced this balance and could continuously adapt to changes? At the end of the day or 1,000 years, "Whatever we do for society and for the world, as a family or as an organization, we have to be worthy of being around for 1,000 years," concluded David.

The above is an example of how you can create long term family legacy plan by setting flexible goals for your business for the benefit of all stakeholders. I know that a 1,000-year legacy plan is too far in the horizon for most business owners, so I will share with you a story about one of my clients in New York, a century-old business, who decided to sell due to family conflicts, and how they went about it to secure a strategic corporate buyer to ensure a win-win situation for all parties involved.

The business owner transition from the first to the second generation went very well because it was simple from her great-grandfather to her grandfather. For the first twenty-five years, the business was small, but the business grew over time. When it came time to transition from the second to the third generation, things got difficult because there were four siblings; their families were involved, and they ended up with four different family silos. It is often easier to transition from the first to the second generation, but as families grow, often they could benefit from having experienced advisors providing them with good governance to manage family conflicts.

This owner decided to sell her business due to family conflicts and profit margin reductions because of the health care industry consolidation. Luckily, the business was successfully purchased at a competitive market value by a large corporation because it was a right strategic acquisition for the buyer. This is an example of how sometimes even the best family legacy plans get derailed due to family conflicts and industry consolidations. Nonetheless, it is imperative to continue to operate the business in a responsible manner to minimize losses and to create a win-win situation for all stakeholders. I hope that the ideas and stories shared in this chapter have inspired you to create your family business legacy plan with a clear vision and peace of mind.

5

FRAME YOUR OUTCOME WITH FAMILY MEMBERS AND TRUSTED ADVISORS

"The most important thing in communication is hearing what isn't said."

— PETER DRUCKER

In this chapter, we will explore ways in which you can create a family business legacy plan, and you will no longer be worried about losing money due to irresponsible choices. Based on my research and experience working with family business owners, it is advisable to frame your desired outcome with family members and advisors and to select a timeframe to accomplish the desired outcome. The business owner with the guidance of her advisors needs to identify the family members who will contribute to the creation of the legacy plan that is equitable and fair for everyone involved including family, non-family members, and other stakeholders. Knowing what negotiable versus non-negotiable considerations are critical and will provide a clear path when making critical decisions because you may not be able to please everybody equally.

While researching business owners and high net worth individuals for this book, many of my clients believe that a defined succession plan is an important success factor of a family business legacy and, most importantly, a crucial factor to maintaining a good family atmosphere, maintaining the family unity and avoiding disputes in which everyone loses. Some entrepreneurs may find it easy to allocate family and business assets while others may find the process challenging. Here is an example of how a business owner and successful entrepreneur who lives in Brazil distributed the family and business assets based on family dynamics. This entrepreneur has two daughters who are not interested and do not feel comfortable making investment decisions. On the other hand, his son who is an economist, feels comfortable and enjoys making business and investment decisions. Since both daughters have a lot of confidence and admiration for their brother, the entrepreneur nominated his son to be his successor. It was a natural family decision; the family and business assets were fairly allocated, and all the family members accepted and were happy with the family estate plan legacy.

A question that is often asked by entrepreneurs is how to identify the challenges and the opportunities for the various stakeholders including, clients, family members, and advisors. Here is another example of how you can train your sons and/or daughters for family succession. Charles, a Harvard Business School OPM32 graduate and a very successful entrepreneur in Brazil, shared with me that a couple of years ago, after his son Felipe left a high-level position at a well-known international bank to become an entrepreneur, Charles provided his son Felipe with detailed business and financial information. Charles also started to train Felipe and ask Felipe for this opinion before making important business or financial decisions. If Charles and Felipe had different points of view on a particular investment opportunity, they discussed the opportunities in depth before making any decisions. The entrepreneur's intention was threefold.

1. To train his son to be his successor
2. To know his son better in a business environment
3. To have his son learn how the entrepreneur thinks in a business environment

This entrepreneur also made his son his partner in new ventures (one at a time). His son earned ownership through "sweat equity shares" in three separate startups in which the entrepreneur was directly involved. Additionally, the entrepreneur was coaching his daughters, who were not interested in the business, and working with them on different projects of mutual interest.

Those children who join their parents' business to provide business continuity because of desire and skillset have been found to be strong performers and effective entrepreneurial leaders and they are able to grow the business in sales and profitability. However, those who join their parents' business due to obligation would more probably not be as successful and instead create family conflicts due to lack of interest and long-term resentment. Therefore, it is important for the family business owner to build mechanisms to develop and articulate the aspirations of each individual member to create a shared family dream because the next generation members' dreams and aspirations may be different from those of the family enterprise. For example, Warren Buffet, one of the wealthiest men in the world and the Chairman, CEO, and president of Berkshire Hathaway, is known for not wanting to spoil his kids and encourages them to follow their passion and be the best they can be by pursuing their God-given talents.

Claudio Fernández-Aráoz, executive fellow at Harvard Business School, reminds us that carefully identifying and properly developing the next generation of leaders is by far the most consequential decision for any family business founder, owner, or leader.

Most business owners consider only one person (will he or she make a great CEO?), rather than thinking of many key family members and the multiple critical potential roles they can play. What's more, even among those leaders who want to conduct rigorous assessments of the entire next generation's capabilities, most don't know what they should focus on, and many wait until the eleventh hour to ask the crucial questions. Claudio Fernández-Aráoz advocates that business leaders need to embrace best practices for talent management, which inevitably require selectivity. Decisions should be based not on experience or even current competencies or abilities, but on the leadership potential of key family members.

According to Claudio Fernández-Aráoz, leadership requirements are changing at an unprecedented rate so leaders must be able to adapt. Business owners should carefully and separately assess the four hallmarks of potential – curiosity, insight, engagement, and determination – to identify those individuals who will be better able to learn and grow and then work obsessively to retain, motivate, and develop them. The earlier you start the process, the better. Once you have identified the personal, individual potential of each of your next generation's most promising family members, the final step will be to candidly share this perspective with them in order to learn their motivation to fill various roles. Personal and family circumstances, as well as individual preferences and identity issues, will make some opt for a full-time executive job while others might prefer the road to a more limited yet still essential part-time contribution. Understanding how far each person can go in certain areas of the business and discovering which roles they are prepared and eager to play will drastically help you strengthen your family's bonds, which will help attract, retain, and develop the best leaders for the business from within and outside the family. Just as important, you will be giving your children the chance to live happier lives in which they become leaders and achieve impact and purpose in unique ways.

As I was gathering information to write this book, I asked business owners if they were successful in creating and implementing a fair and equitable family business legacy plan. If so, what made it fair and equitable and how did they feel about it? Most of them responded that although challenging, they had created a fair and equitable family business legacy plan and felt at peace with their decisions. One of the most notable responses came from Pablo, a Harvard Business School OPM32 graduate and a successful entrepreneur in Argentina, who responded: "Each of my kids will inherit the same percentage of my wealth. In the future, they will need to decide if they continue to be partners or if they are going to split the wealth. I do not have nor do I want to have any control of this. I have always taught my children by example, business sense, ethics, and values. If that is not enough, I failed."

Should you create your family business legacy plan yourself or should you hire advisors to help you in the process? In my experience, most entrepreneurs who have successfully completed their family business legacy plan have worked with their trusted advisors. Although legacy plans may be similar, we know that there are not two-family business succession plans that are equal, because they are highly personal and they vary based on the overall family dynamics. If it is not clear what the business owner wants or if he never thought about succession planning, I strongly recommended that he hire a specialized advisor. A business owner should never put in place a succession plan without checking the implications of it with his family members, advisors, tax accountants, attorneys, and other important stakeholders.

The great secret of business families that achieve tremendous wealth and hold onto it for generations is that they persistently promote the entrepreneurial spirit that led to their initial success. That drive – a combination of ambition, sheer will, and the willingness to take calculated risks – is integral to long-term success, particularly in challenging times. While there is no right path to creating a sustainable entrepreneurial drive, in business families, successful ventures do have common threads. They foster the right attitude in future generations by focusing on several core principles such as sharing the hard reality of the business challenges, establishing mutual ground rules, supporting aspiring entrepreneurs who want to flourish on their own, and providing encouragement without micromanaging. In their article, "Is the Next Generation of Your Family Business Entrepreneurial Enough?" Judy Lin Walsh, Sam Bruehl, and Nick Di Loreto note that these principles highlight how important it is to find the balance between offering wisdom and dictating how something must be done so that you stoke the next generation's entrepreneurial fire. No matter how great the founding idea or business is, it cannot last indefinitely. Business families need fresh infusions of entrepreneurial drive and passion to adapt to changing environments so they continue to thrive. And family business members need to test their mettle and be driven to succeed on their own for their sense of self-worth.

In my experience, when creating a family business legacy plan, another strong motivator is to create a legacy plan that takes into consideration what the business owner wants or needs for income long-term. For instance, if the owner decides to sell the business, figuring out the seller's desired income can be a good place to work back from when trusted advisors are determining how to best structure a tax-efficient sale. Sales can be structured with various types of trusts as parting gifts; stock sales versus asset sales; sales involving nonqualified deferred compensation, dividend policies, long-term leases, and consulting agreements. Another consideration is how much control or involvement the seller would like once the business is sold. In general, the seller is better off if the sale is a stock or ownership interest. Also, for tax purposes, the seller may want to sell the business in installments over time or gift part of the business to family members, both of which can reduce taxes. As always, there is a caveat on taxation, especially at the time of writing this book in March 2021. In the United States, President Biden's administration is proposing significant changes to estate planning suggested in the proposed new legislation entitled: "For the 99.5 Percent Act." The Act significantly reduces the federal estate and gift tax exemptions. It also eliminates as early as the date of enactment many of the estate planning techniques used by estate planers while other provisions changes would generally be effective as of December 31, 2021. The estate tax exemption under the Act would move to $3,500,000 down from the current exemption of $11,700,000. The Act would also reduce the lifetime gift tax exemption to $1,000,000. Under the Act, the estate and gift tax rates, which are currently up to 40 percent, are also scheduled to increase to a range from 45 percent to 65 percent. If "For the 99.5 Percent Act" is enacted, it could cause significant changes in the approach to family legacy and estate planning.

According to an article on estate and inheritance taxes around the world written by Alan Cole and published in the *Tax Foundation*, the nation's leading independent tax policy, the United States is one of many countries that levies taxes on estates or inheritances. This report compares this aspect of the U.S. tax system to other countries around the world and examines recent worldwide trends in estate and inheritance taxes. The highest top estate tax rate to lineal heirs can be found in Japan at 55 percent. South Korea (50 percent) and France (45 percent) also have rates higher than the U.S. At the low end, fifteen of the thirty-four countries in the Organization for Economic Cooperation and Development (OECD) have no taxes on property passed to lineal heirs. The average estate tax rate across the OECD is 15 percent with a median tax rate of 7 percent.

In summary, considering the higher estate exemption available as of June 2021 in the United States and the ability to use some of the estate planning techniques that would be eliminated in the Act, now is the time to talk to your tax and trusted advisors to be sure you understand the tax and cashflow consequences of using your gift exemption during your life while the higher exemptions are still available. Act now and start talking with your trusted advisors to create a family business legacy plan, and you will no longer be worried about losing money due to irresponsible choices.

6

ENVISION YOUR SUCCESS

"Efficiency is doing things right; effectiveness is doing the right things."

— PETER DRUCKER

In this chapter, you will envision your success by identifying and prioritizing business products and/or services based on profitability as well as making sure that the business records are accurate. Therefore, an annual audit must be performed by a reputable CPA firm to enable you to protect your company from employee theft and to increase the accuracy of the business accounting records. The annual audit results are reported in a written audit opinion and the language in the opinion defines an audit. An auditor reports on several topics including financial statements, regulatory requirements, and internal controls because stakeholders including investors, creditors, and regulators rely on the accuracy of the financial statements.

Rapid growth may cause an owner to lose control of operations, and business efficiency and profitability can decline. An audit reveals areas of company inefficiency and helps the owner to make improvements. It should be noted that there is a difference between a financial audit versus a forensic audit. The financial audit looks to determine your company's financial health for its current or potential investors and other stakeholders. The forensic audit is performed to provide support with litigation, and they can also conduct an internal control examination to identify potential opportunities for employees to manipulate current company controls to misappropriate funds or assets from the company.

As an entrepreneur, you will need to evaluate your business and decide what products are profitable, what products are not profitable – if any – and what products complement profitable products or services. Evaluate and decide to no longer offer products/services that are not profitable. It should be noted that most companies today struggle with identifying which of their offerings and which of their customers are the most profitable. They can measure revenue but not the profit associated with the product or customer(s), which means they make decisions about what to sell in which markets to which customers and at what price based on partial or inaccurate information. Methods used to allocate large buckets of costs such as sales, advertising, and customer service can be arbitrary and potentially inaccurate. Are some of the less profitable products and/or services complementary to the profitability of your business?

Therefore, analyzing your overall business, evaluating where sales are coming from, who are your best and most profitable clients, talking to them, and soliciting their feedback is important for the growth of your business. As a business owner, you need to engage your clients in the conversation of the future of your company and show appreciation for their business. According to McKenley Advisors, it is important to understand and measure products and services against three metrics – profitability, stakeholder behavior, and perceived value and staff perceptions. And with that understanding in place, determining a clear path for future investment and product prioritization becomes straightforward.

The most important metrics that a business owner must focus on are sales revenue, gross and net profit margin, and monthly recurring revenue. The best way to grow your sales revenue is to increase the number of sales by expanding your marketing, hiring new salespeople, or making special discount offers. Gross margins can be improved by making both your sales and production processes more efficient and monitor your sales growth over various time periods – monthly, yearly, and long-term metrics will give you a better understanding of where your company stands. Make it a goal to accelerate your sales growth every month or at least keep it at the same percentage month after month. Evaluating the customer lifetime value of various client segments can help you understand which segments bring in a higher profit. Let go of clients who are decreasing your net profit and difficult to convert and focus on the most rewarding clients and prospects. Having loyal customers is beneficial in many ways. It helps to grow your sales and spread the word about your products and/or services, and customer loyalty can be increased over time by providing excellent customer care and delivering high-quality products. Happy stakeholders and staff lead to long-term commitment and profitability. Business owners with a long-term and clear vision keep all stakeholders including family and non-family members motivated and involved in the growth and profitability of the business.

In a *Harvard Business Review* article, Werner Reinartz and Wolfgang Ulaga write about how to sell services more profitably. When products become commodities, manufacturing companies may seek to differentiate themselves with value-added services – a potentially profitable strategy. Unfortunately, companies often stumble in the effort. Reinartz and Ulaga conducted in-depth studies of eighteen leading companies in a broad variety of product markets to learn what distinguished the successes from the rest. They discovered four steps to developing a profitable services capability.

1. Recognize that you already have a service company. You can identify and charge for simple services – as Merck did when it stopped quietly absorbing shipping costs.
2. Switching services from free to fee

clarifies their value for managers as well as for customers.

3. Industrialize the back office. To prevent delivery costs from eating up service-offering margins, build flexible service platforms, closely monitor process costs, and exploit new technologies that enable process innovations. The Swedish bearings manufacturer SKF provided off-site access to an online monitoring tool that could warn of potential failure in customers' machines.

4. Create a service-savvy sales force by focusing on customers' satisfaction and the opportunities for new service offerings. Schneider-Electric did a major overhaul of its sales organization and trained its people to switch from cost-plus pricing to value-based pricing. You may need to acquire new capabilities to take advantage of those opportunities. The industrial coatings specialist PPG had to learn how painting robots function after it offered to take over Fiat's Torino paint shop. Services can both lock in customers and help acquire new accounts. They

should be developed with care and attention.

In the book *Manage for Profit, Not for Market Share: A Guide to Greater Profits in Highly Contested Markets* the authors Hermann Simon, Frank F. Bilstein, and Frank Luby point out that the importance of challenging and changing your existing assumptions about your customers is the most important first step in identifying your hidden profit opportunities. It is always easier to retool by assuming what your customers want and are willing to pay versus retooling based on actual data. The authors explain the dangers inherent in using gut feeling, anecdotal evidence, and other corporate shortcuts to guide your decision making and use the links between price and profit to demonstrate the advantages of data-driven analysis.

In the article *Pricing Strategy and the Net*, the authors Leyland F. Pitt, Pierre Berthon, Richard T. Watson, and Michael Ewing write about marketing mix variables and how pricing directly affects a firm's revenue. The advent of a new medium for buyer-seller interaction, the internet, is changing the issue of price for both customers and suppliers in an unprecedented way. On one hand, there are internet dynamics that flatten the customer value pyramid (defined by the value of the customer to the firm) because of technology that facilitates customer search, customer control over transactions, the provision of means by which the customer can make rather than take the price, a return to one-on-one negotiation, and commoditization of markets. Countervailing dynamics of the internet enable the firm in some instances to differentiate pricing all the time, to create customer switching barriers, to "de-menu" pricing, to differentiate on other dimensions of the purchase decision, and to reduce transaction costs. It is important to understand the internet-based pricing dynamics and price your products and/or services according to the relative strengths of buyer and seller. These dynamics suggest that pricing decisions can be as creative as those made about the development of new products and services or advertising campaigns. According to this article, pricing may be indeed the last frontier for marketing creativity.

During my research for this book, I also interviewed business owners who have fast-growing companies operating in an uncertain economic, political, and unstable countries with a weak currency. One of these entrepreneurs is Pablo C., a

Harvard Business School OPM32 graduate who owns an investment company in Argentina. Pablo is in the process of restructuring his company to operate outside Argentina to provide more stability and profitability with hard currency revenues. Understanding what products and/or services are profitable is critical to the overall profitability of the company.

Creating and managing a fast-growing company in an unstable environment is risky because the business owner can easily lose track of the finances. Brian Hamilton, chairman of financial information company Sageworks says, "When your business is smaller, you probably have a pretty good command of your numbers. You can watch your cash and know quickly how expenses are stacking up to sales. But once you get to a certain sales range, it's hard to keep track of your financials in your head."

You must keep track of your budget and understand your cash flow, which are key factors in managing a fast-growing business. Brian suggests consulting with your accountant more often than just during tax season since cash flow mistakes are some of the main reasons why businesses fail. Also, overly optimistic growth projections or the failure to understand the difference between revenue, net profit, and actual cash on hand can mean trouble for your business. Fast-paced growth can be dangerous for your company if you do not go about it the right way. Do not lose track of your finances, and make sure that functions such as customer service, technology, and business operations are built to scale. For instance, an entrepreneur who has a small business in an unstable socio-economic country may be better off selling his company.

It should be noted that there would not be many opportunistic buyers in a country with a weak currency and unstable economy; however, the entrepreneur may want to engage her employees in the conversation of the future of the company and sell the company through the Employee Stock Ownership Plan (ESOP). Since most employees do not have enough cash to purchase company stock outright, the ESOP would give the employees permission to take out a commercial loan and purchase the stock. A commercial lender would likely approve the ESOP loan because the collateral on the loan would be the stock assets and goodwill of the company. The employees would then have to make monthly payments to the lender just like with any other loan. If this is possible, it will enable the entrepreneur to sell her company at a competitive price and create an estate plan to distribute the money or make a trust to the benefit of his family.

I have shared ideas about identifying and prioritizing your business products and services based on the profitability including knowing when to sell a business that is no longer profitable due to government legislation and market conditions outside your control. Remember that according to Peter Drucker, "Efficiency is doing things right; effectiveness is doing the right things."

7

CHALLENGES AND OPPORTUNITIES – TO SELL OR NOT TO SELL?

"Communication – the human connection – is the key to personal and career success"

— PAUL MEYER

In this chapter, we will talk about how best to identify the various business challenges and opportunities. Think about some of your business challenges and opportunities. An opportunity could be deciding whether to sell or not sell your business. The time to sell is when the owner is ready, the business is ready, and the market is ready. Most business owners wait too long to start thinking about the transition, and as a result, they end up selling their life-long effort for less than they could have if they had planned things earlier. As a *Harvard Business Review* article argues, "These are scary times for business owners and managers due to the increasing danger of disruptive change. The nature of work is changing and new technology and product innovation from your competition may drastically affect your business."

If you decide to sell your business, here are some questions to ask yourself to set up a successful exit plan. Exit planning is a vital part of the lifecycle of a business. If you are planning to stay involved in the business, how much control do you want after your exit?

In my survey, I found out that over 90 percent of business owners agree that a transition strategy is important to maximize return on your equity. Think about how you plan to replace yourself. You must find ways to train either family or non-family members to take over your day-to-day responsibilities. Have you done a valuation of your business? Are your records ready to justify your desired asking price? Knowing how much your business is worth is critically important to maximize your future after tax dollars. You need to expand your strategic planning to include contingency planning, succession planning, and transition planning. If you were to sell your business, what is next for you? What will new life look like? Would you like to travel, spend more time with your family, start a new hobby, do charitable work in alignment with your values? The possibilities are endless. If you are ready, have fun creating your future self.

According to the article in the *Harvard Business Review*, the main challenges and opportunities of organizational behavior are improving peoples' skills, improving quality and productivity, total quality management, managing workforce diversity, responding to globalization, empowering people, coping with temporariness, stimulating innovation and change, emergence of e-organization and e-commerce, improving ethical behavior, improving customer service, helping employees balance work-life conflicts, and flattening world. These are some of the reasons why Lin, a Harvard Business School OPM32 graduate and successful entrepreneur operating in Atlanta, decided to sell the business. After multiple conversations with his family – of whom two are active in the business – neither felt as if they would like to wake up in the morning and be responsible for the well-being of 2,500 employees. Their option would also be to expand the senior management team and become passive shareholders.

However, they did not like the risk of not being active operating managers. Therefore, after further consideration and in consultation with trusted advisors, Lin decided to start liquidating his US operations and to start a family investment office. This entrepreneur and his family are now also focusing their efforts on communication to prevent conflicts and preserving relationships with family members and key stakeholders, governance to ensure the right structures and procedures are in place within the family for future success, and preparing successors to lead effectively and assume new roles in the family investment office with confidence. The family office will be the wealth legacy that requires family involvement. In the evaluation of the children, Lin recognized that his oldest daughter was the best at negotiating settlements between the siblings, as the business owner has seven children ranging in age from forty to four. With the widespread age difference of the stakeholders, the wealth is currently disproportionate, as the older children have already received a portion of their shares. The younger children will be funded at certain age restrictions, or the shares will reside in their trust. It is interesting to note that this entrepreneur's preference would have been the German model and to hire outside senior management, such as managing director, COO, and CEO, and to allow the company to continue with the family receiving distributions from the operating companies. However, as a family, they chose not to do this after a full evaluation of the risk profile.

In this chapter's discussion of whether to sell or not to sell your business, I will also share with you Adriana's story, a business owner in Florida who was faced with a major challenge when she realized that her company had not invested the time, talent, or money in innovating, improving the technology of its online business, creating new products, and/or improving the products or services being sold to their clients.

Adriana's clients had not increased over five years, yet the company remained profitable due to its healthy operating margins. Adriana was considering selling her business because she had received offers to purchase her business from her competitors. However, after doing a business valuation and consulting with her family and advisors, she realized that she could increase the valuation of her company by acquiring new and maintaining old clients to increase sales and income by encouraging family and non-family members to think about how best to improve existing products or to create new products and genuinely welcome new and innovative ideas.

Adriana provided the younger generation with opportunities to learn and encouraged experimentation and innovation. Working with advisors and family members, Adriana created a corporate governance structure to have a mix of family and non-family members with diverse backgrounds and experiences create a working environment to promote and encourage new ideas and seek opportunities for outside alliances and collaboration to increase learning and the creation of new technology and product ideas. This business owner also decided to tap the talents and ideas of family and non-family members who were engaged and committed to growing the company through innovation. Adriana provided open access to information and ample rewards and recognition, and she also took advantage of new business and financial partners to utilize the knowledge she did not have and to spread the financial risk. She created a separate organization because this innovation venture would require greater financial risk, the larger time horizon for creation, and experimentation as well as family collaboration. One of the first things that this new organization resolved to do was a survey of their existing clients and prospects to gather ideas and to find out what was working and what areas needed improvement and establish the time frame to accomplish and measure the success or failure of each identified innovative goal(s).

In their book, *Entrepreneurs in Every Generation*, Allan R. Cohen and Pramodita Sharma specify the conditions supporting entrepreneurial and innovative behavior. Based on their research, they share companies' experiences with three different levels of innovation – incremental innovation, where people at every level are making frequent minor adjustments to everyday problems while doing their work; progressive innovation, the application of a known tool or technique to adjacent territories which has often led to new products, the extension of existing business lines, and a new application of existing technology to a different area; and breakthrough or radical renovations, which are those where an entirely new industry, product category, or way of doing business is created and sustained.

If a business owner wants to create a fertile environment for entrepreneurship and innovation, she should, on an ongoing basis, set aside discretionary funds outside the regular operating budget for innovation. The owner should encourage and expect that everyone contributes innovative ideas at all levels as part of their jobs and have constant expectations of high improving performance with no penalties for failures. The owner should empower her employees to think holistically, to take reasonable risks, and reduce segmentation and boundaries between units. The owner should also have open access to information and ample rewards and recognition. Innovation keeps the business moving forward and often, there are research and development (R&D) tax credits to fund these innovations. Depending on the nature and the timing of these innovations, a business owner could take advantage of these R&D tax credits. Some of these tax credits incentivize businesses to undertake specific types of research and development including development of new, improved, or more reliable products, processes, and techniques.

In conclusion, there are many challenges and opportunities available to business owners. In this chapter, I shared with you examples of two business owners, one business owner decided it was time to sell her business and another business owner decided to bring her business to the next level of sales and profitability through innovation. Each of them made their decision based on their overall personal and business objectives.

8

BUSINESS OWNERSHIP AND LEGACY

"In character, in manner, in style, in all things, the supreme excellence is simplicity."

— HENRY WADSWORTH LONGFELLOW

In this chapter, we will think through and consult with trusted advisors about the best way to structure business ownership and create a business legacy. The most common forms of business ownership are sole proprietorship, partnership, limited liability partnership, limited liability company (LLC), series LLC, and corporations, which can be taxed as C corporations or S corporations. These are all different forms of ownership and selecting the right type of business ownership varies depending on the mission and vision of the business.

Among the different business structures, a sole proprietorship is the simplest form of business ownership. Apart from being a common preference by business owners, it is also owned solely by an individual. It is an unincorporated business owned and run by one individual with no distinction between the business and the owner. The business owner is entitled to all profits and is responsible for all the business's debts, losses, and liabilities. Some of the main advantages of a sole proprietorship are having no boss, easy and inexpensive to form, complete control, and easy tax preparation. Some of the disadvantages include unlimited personal liability because there is no legal separation between the sole proprietor and the business, the proprietor can be held personally liable for the debts and obligations of the business including any liabilities incurred as a result of employee actions, it is hard to raise money because of the perceived additional risk when it comes to repayment if the business fails, and the proprietor is responsible for the failure of the business. When it comes to taxes, because the proprietor and the business are one and the same, the business itself is not taxed separately. The sole proprietorship income is the taxable income. The income and/or losses and expenses are reported with a Schedule C and the standard Form 1040. You can find more information about sole proprietorship, taxes, and forms at IRS.gov.

The main reason for forming a limited liability company or corporation is to limit the liability of the owners. In a sole proprietorship or partnership, the owners are personally liable for the debts and liabilities of the business. Also, creditors can go after all of their assets (business and personal) to collect. If an LLC is formed and operated properly, the owners can be protected from such liability. The creditors can take the bank accounts, cars, real estate, and other property of any partner to pay the debts of the partnership. If only one partner has money, he or she may have to pay all of the debts accumulated by all the other partners. When doing business as an LLC, the company may go bankrupt and the members may lose their initial investment, but the creditors cannot touch the assets of the owners. The limited liability company offers the greatest benefits when compared to partnerships and sole proprietorships. Most partnerships and sole proprietorships often switch to an LLC.

Some of the advantages of the LLC include

continuous existence, limited liability, ease of transferability, sharing ownership, ease of raising capital, and ease estate planning. A limited liability company may have a perpetual existence. When a sole proprietor or partner dies, the assets of his or her business may go to his or her heirs, but the business may no longer exist. If the surviving spouse or other heirs of a business owner want to continue the business in their names, it will be considered a new business – even if they are using the assets of the old business. With a partnership, the death of one partner may cause a dissolution of the business.

If a member of a limited liability company does something negligent, signs a debt personally, or guarantees a company debt, the limited liability company will not protect him or her from the consequences of his or her own act or from the debt. Also, if a limited liability company does not follow the proper formalities, it may be ignored by a court and the owners or officers may be held personally liable. The formalities include having separate bank accounts, filing annual reports, and following other requirements of state law.

A limited liability company and all its assets and accounts may be transferred by the simple assignment of an interest in the company. With a sole proprietorship, each of the individual assets must be transferred and the accounts, licenses, and permits must be individually transferred. With a limited liability company, the owner of a business can share the profits of a business without giving up control. This is done by setting up the share of profits separate from the share of ownership.

A limited liability company may raise capital by admitting new members or borrowing money. In most cases, a business does not pay taxes on money it raises by the sale of its shares. An LLC has all its own bank accounts and records. A partner or sole proprietor may have trouble differentiating which of his or her expenses were for business and which were for personal items. With an LLC or corporation, ownership of the company can be distributed more easily than with a partnership or sole proprietorship. Different beneficiaries can be given different percentages and control can be limited to those who are most capable. This is done by having different classes of ownership, different distribution of profits, and different levels of control. Death taxes can be minimized or avoided if small amounts of ownership are transferred tax-free each year before death. As always, consult with your tax expert because the IRS rules must be followed carefully.

Some of the disadvantages are the cost of creating a limited liability company (LLC) in comparison with creating a sole proprietor or a partnership. A limited liability company owner may have to pay unemployment compensation for herself, which she would not have to pay as a sole proprietor. Also, a business owner must keep her personal business separate from the business of the limited liability company. The limited liability company must have its own records and money must be kept separate.

Ray, a Harvard Business School OPM32 business owner in Boston who I interviewed for this book, created various companies with different types of business ownership to take advantage of the tax laws and to accommodate his family business legacy. This entrepreneur has three daughters and wanted to make sure that they all had an opportunity to run and own businesses which included real estate. I was impressed when I interviewed Ray because he had created a family charter or protocol to enable the family to be united in their decision-making and to promote both short- and long-term family business goals. The family charter specifies rules, responsibilities, and obligations relating to the ownership and management of the companies as well as the values that will guide family members' conduct in the community. This savvy business owner created an effective family charter that captured important benefits, both tangible and intangible, to facilitate a smooth process for leadership succession – a tangible benefit. Ray knows that not creating a well-established and codified formal plan for succession may produce disastrous consequences for a family business. Therefore, he created and maintains a family business legacy through family charter provisions that promote family unity and affiliation. Philanthropy and other joint activities have, over the last thirty years, promoted family cohesion and bonding.

According to the Boston Consulting Group, a comprehensive family charter covers the following seven topics. A family charter provides clear guidance and can relieve the stress of the new generation. It should specify the term of the charter and a process for revisions, including how long the charter will remain in effect and how the term can be extended or renewed as well as the process for amending or adding provisions to the charter. It also specifies the philanthropic or other local, regional, and global joint activities that the business should promote and thus creates family cohesion and bonding.

A family charter also stipulates the family members' succession and involvement in the business and the principles that will guide the leadership succession process and how family members' performance will be evaluated and compensated.

It will also establish guidelines for management of business ownership and what restrictions and incentives should be in place to keep ownership of the business within the family. A family charter addresses governance and how the family should be organized and governed to achieve its vision and promote its values. As businesses and their families evolve over time, the governance structure must also be reexamined and renewed based on family values and market environment. It will also identify the family core values and vision for its role in the broader community. Philanthropy helps build relationships with clients and potential clients. It helps build and support the business brand. It promotes employee engagement and good corporate citizens want to do business with others who share their values. A family charter should specify who is considered a family member. Traditionally, family is a group of persons related to one another by blood or marriage, or a group of parents and children living together in a household. There is no one right way to define family. Family could be a group of people affiliated through bonds of shared history and commitment to share a future together while supporting the development and well-being of individual members. In some instances, the leadership role is passed on to the daughter or son-in-law. For instance, at Walmart, a large family-controlled company, Gregg Penner, the grandson-in-law of Walmart founder Sam Walton, took over as the Chairman of the Board from his father-in-law Rob Walton in 2015.

According to my Harvard Business School professor John Davis, a family or a non-family member, whether within a family enterprise or outside it, can be an effective CEO. Also, with more women in business, we are seeing more women involved in their family business's day to day management, such Abigail Johnson at Fidelity Investments in Boston and Delphine Arnault at Louis Vuitton in France.

A family charter will also address governance and how the family should be organized and governed to achieve its vision and promote its values. In their book, *Entrepreneurs in Every Generation*, Allan Cohen and Pramodita Sharma provide us with a set of propositions that will help the family members with governance, including but not limited to the following: building influence upon reciprocity and exchange and respect for the stakeholders even when you disagree with them. It is important to understand the why behind the disagreement to explore new and more creative ideas. Start with what is in it for those you wish to influence, for example, preserving the future of the company. Try every new goal as a pilot project, create data, learn from it and adjust as you go, and involve others to help with the project. Emphasize the opportunity to learn rather than how this will prove others should have learned. Learn from differences of opinions. Provide service to the business of family that no one else wants to do to build credibility. Outwork everyone; it will be noticed. Participate in interesting family business conferences that you can jointly attend. Look for influential allies, get to know them, find common ground, always be looking to what you can do for them. Be thoughtful, kind, and generous to everyone in the company. Enterprising families value the "we" over the "I."

I know that the most important part of transitioning a family business is to have a well-thought out, defined, and clearly communicated plan for both family and non-family members. The plan may change over time and as the business evolves but, in the meantime, everyone will be able to know the business' goals and objectives. In my experience, it is important to separate business life from family life – discuss business decisions at the office and enjoy family discussions around the dinner table.

I have seen mistakes families make that lead to broken businesses. However, it is often preventable if the owner runs the business as "business first" and "family second." This is not to say that the business is more important than the family; instead, it means that the business owner loves and honors the family, and she is going to properly manage the business to ensure the financial security and well-being of the family.

Of course, communication is key, and although some family members may not like some policies and procedures, they deserve to know the rules of engagement in the family business and then they can decide whether they want to be part of the family business or not. Keep in mind that there are advisors that can help the family business owner to work things out with her family members and stake-holders as well as to properly structure the business and establish policies and procedures to create a family business legacy.

I shared with you various way to structure business ownership and create a business legacy, and you must now select and decide along with your trusted advisors which of these business ownerships will enable you to accomplish your unique family business legacy.

9

ENVISION AND CREATE YOUR MASTERPIECE

"Remember that happiness is a decision, not a result."

— DAN SULLIVAN

In this chapter, I will provide you with ideas about creating and implementing your business legacy that is in alignment with your values. Most business owners do not have a clear vision as to when and how they should create a family business legacy; therefore, they often wait until it is too late, and they end up paying an enormous amount of money on taxes. Creating the right foundation for your family business legacy is a long-term project based on the values of the entrepreneur and allowing space for each generation to find their passion. Accordingly, each family member must earn their place within the organization and needs to be compensated accordingly, either with tangible or intangible benefits. One of the entrepreneur's delicate tasks is to regularly apply the family values and to properly train each generation according to their passions and talents and within the organization's mission and vision.

In the process of writing this book, I contacted some of my global Harvard Business School friends and classmates, and my research shows that some of the Harvard Business School Owner President Management (OPM) graduates have decided to give away a percentage of the company ownership to their children during life and teach their children how to be responsible for what they receive now and could receive in the future. These business owners felt that giving during life makes their children legally responsible and desire to do the right things for the organization and for themselves to preserve a family business legacy.

Another important factor is that these business owners surrounded themselves with competent advisors such as lawyers, tax advisors, and family members to come up with a successful business legacy plan. Also, an important aspect of this business plan is for their children to work in the business, and the family succession has been well received by the business stakeholders since they see continuity and fresh blood with new ideas. The decision to create and implement family business succession for these entrepreneurs is the fact that they own 100 percent of the company shares and want to keep business ownership within the family. Also, they feel responsible and want to protect the well-being of all their employees and respect their hopes and dreams which are based on the success of the business. They also believe that inheriting the family business is not a property right, but a responsibility. These business owners also believe that the most important issues are how to train and educate children born in wealth and being careful how not to spoil them by helping them develop strong self-esteem, good values, and reasonable hunger. Also, a bond that holds the family together is being transparent, generous, and letting each child be what he or she dreams to be; supporting family members and providing a safe place to deal with personal and business conflicts; and learning from mistakes.

There are many different legacy models, but the most important consideration is to create a legacy model that works for your family. Therefore, having a clear understanding of how to address potentially contentious issues and having a mechanism in place to allocate decision rights and responsibilities among the family members are critically important to sustain its success and preserve the business legacy for generations to come. One thing that I found most interesting about these business owners is that they and the members of their families believe that they are only keepers of the tangible wealth and intangible goodwill created by their business and that it is their responsibility to preserve, maintain, and make the company grow until they pass the family business to the next generation. Pablo, a Harvard Business School OPM32 graduate and a successful business owner in Argentina, believes that "they are not business owners, but the momentary keepers of planetary jewels." This understanding of property and businesses creates a smooth business succession, and the key to family business legacy is the family values and the education of the next generation.

To create a clear vision for the business planning and continued success of the company, the business owner must reflect on the past, look at the present, and visualize the future to create an inspiring vision for the company. This vision will be a road map for its management, employees, and family members to actively participate and execute the business succession plan. It takes a team of many individuals to create and achieve a shared vision. The company's vision creates a beginning point and a destination; the business plan sets the goals, objectives and the strategies and tactics to achieve them. You must recruit the best leaders, managers, and employees that share the same passion and desire to be the best. Leadership identifies the best managers and then invests in training those with drive and potential.

For many business owners, operating their business day-to-day is time-consuming and retirement seems distant. However, establishing a sound family business succession plan is beneficial and necessary, and it requires careful preparation. Business owners seeking a smooth and equitable transition of their interests should seek competent and experienced advisors to help with the business for transition and create and help implement strategies to maximize the benefits and minimize both business and personal taxes. Some of the steps that a business owner needs to consider in transitioning out include evaluating the current marketplace and what is happening in the community, throughout the country, and even around the world that might impact a future sale or continuity of the business. It is important to determine the current growth of the business, changes in technology, and changes in the industry overall.

Creating a family business legacy plan that is in alignment with the business owner's values is not easy, but once you decide to proceed, is relatively easy if you surround yourself with financial, business, and tax advisors to guide you and avail yourself with alternatives based on your individual situation. While some business owners decide to provide continuity to the family business, others may decide to sell their family business. Some of my clients have sold the company through an employee stock ownership plan (ESOP). An ESOP can be used to create a market for your shares and provide some tax benefits. Whichever decision you make about your business succession plan, it is critically important to hire an experienced business appraiser to conduct an evaluation of your business and to make sure that there are no liens or encumbrances affecting the continued success of the business. This is a perfect time to review and organize incorporation documents, equity ownership records, and to have all financial statements up to date. The accuracy of the business financial statements will determine the business valuation. If you have family members involved in the business, it is important to get them involved and informed along your planning process.

Ideally, the transition should be a gradual, multi-year process, due to the complexity involved in most business transition plans. For example, if you think you may be ready to exit your business within the next three to five years, now is the time to start that process. While that timeframe surprises some business owners, taking a long-term approach allows for a well-thought-out transition. As you build this transition team, it is important to identify one key advisor who can take a lead role in the process and coordinate efforts for a smoother transition. Although you may have specific goals for business growth and profitability, planning for various outcomes can help you be prepared for any contingency. Your financial models should contemplate several different contingencies, and your transition plan should be designed around more than one potential outcome.

Transitioning a business can result in different tax ramifications for the business and its shareholders, depending on how the deal is structured. Here is Helene's example, one of my business owners in

New York City, who after thirty years of running her business, thought about her next phase of her life and decided to get ready to transition her business in the next two to three years. Helene assembled a strong team of advisors including her accountant, tax advisor, and family members to provide advice for both her business and her family, which includes her husband and two sons.

Helene knew that the transition of her business would have estate and tax implications, particularly given her family dynamics. Her older son had worked alongside her in the business for years, whereas her younger son was not as involved in the business. Helene consulted with her team of professionals, and she made sure that her husband and her two sons were a part of the process. The first step for her team was to create estate planning documents and secondly, to think and strategize the business transfer. These included a will, a revocable trust for Helene and her husband, and power of attorney and healthcare documentation. The next step in the estate plan was to incorporate leveraged gifts for their children and grandchildren in the form of grantor retained annuity trust (GRAT), a financial instrument used in estate planning to minimize taxes on large financial gifts to family members. This tax-efficient wealth planning strategy can be accomplished by transferring assets to the GRAT but retaining the right to receive a series of annuity payments from the GRAT for a specified term of years. Each annuity payment is based on a percentage of the fair market value of the assets transferred to the Grantor Retained Annuity Trust (GRAT) determined at the time of transfer. The annuity payments would be satisfied by paying Helene and her husband the income earned by the assets owned by the GRAT and, if the income proved to be insufficient, by returning them a portion of those assets. Any property remaining in the GRAT after all the periodic annuity payments had been made would be distributed to their beneficiaries.

After in-depth discussions about how to plan for and to mitigate estate tax implications, Helene and her husband purchased a second-to-die life insurance policy, which provides benefits to the heirs only after the last surviving spouse dies. In conjunction with this, they also executed an irrevocable life insurance trust, which names a trust and trustee as the beneficiaries of the life insurance policy and includes rules set for the trust. This structure is designed to provide needed liquidity to pay estate taxes.

Because Helene's team was in place, she was able to plan for the sale of her business years in advance. She worked with her advisors and took action to improve metrics on accounts receivable and her return on investment, making the business more attractive to potential buyers. Helene also assembled an excellent management team who would be willing and able to continue in their roles after the sale, helping to ensure continuity in the transition. Also, because Helene's sons were part of the management team, her business transition planning and estate planning often overlapped. By involving her family from the beginning, Helene ensured a smoother transition when the time comes for the sale of the business without risking family harmony.

I hope that these examples have given you estate planning ideas to enable you to create your family business legacy plan that is in alignment with your personal and business values.

10

EXPAND YOUR REACH/DESIGN YOUR PLAN WITH AN END IN MIND!

"Begin with the end in mind."

— STEPHEN COVEY

In this chapter, you will see how many business owners create a family business legacy plan that is fair and equitable. It should be noted that fair and equitable does not necessarily mean equal. While something close to equal is often the result, depending on the circumstances, the division may be unequal depending on the contribution of each of the family members. However, many parents want their children to be treated equally when it comes to family business planning. Parents who are concerned about family harmony are wise to address the issues of estate equalization as a key element of their estate and business planning. Most of the problems that would create disharmony in their children can be handled with careful thought and with wills, trusts, and business agreements that dictate the legacy plan. An important step in a family business legacy plan is to have family meetings to discuss the plans, answer questions from all sides, and reinforce the reasons and strategy behind the planning.

In this chapter, we are going to talk about wills, trusts, and agreements available to create a family business legacy plan and the use of life insurance to accommodate children who have physical or mental disabilities, addictions, or other self-destructive behavior. The insurance is used to create liquidity for any remaining estate assets and to create a legacy for children with disabilities. It is important for the business owner to consult with a legal expert in her jurisdiction before creating a testamentary trust will for a disabled child so as not to disqualify such a child from any government grants or benefits.

A testamentary trust can be used effectively when one or more members of the family warrant special consideration and/or when the beneficiary is not old enough to legally own property and/or not equipped to control or manage the inheritance responsibly. A testamentary trust arises upon the death of the testator, and which is specified in his or her will. A will may contain more than one testamentary trust and may address all or any portion of the estate. Testamentary trusts are distinguished from inter-vivos trusts, which are created during the settlor's lifetime. A business owner can also set up a charitable trust to enable the trustees can make tax-free donations to an eligible school, church, charity, etcetera. A charitable trust is an irrevocable trust established for charitable purposes, and the trust enjoys a varying degree of tax benefits.

When considering life insurance to equalize the estate, there are basically two types of life insurance policies – whole life and term insurance. Whole life insurance is typically more expensive than term life policies, but the premium amount typically does not change throughout the life of the policy. Over time, this helps make whole life insurance more affordable. The payout your beneficiary receives if you die during the coverage period is typically tax-free and has a steady value throughout the life of the policy. If you need to, you can renew your policy when it ends. The premiums can be a bit higher. If needed, you may be able to access your money through loans for an additional charge. You can customize a whole life insurance policy with a variety of riders for an additional charge.

Term insurance is a good option if you want to pay for life insurance during the time when the need is greatest, for example when your kids are younger or while you are paying a mortgage. Term life insurance is available in ten-year, fifteen-year, twenty-year, or thirty-year terms, and is renewable annually. A term policy can be converted to a permanent life insurance policy at the end of the term. The benefits of term insurance include guaranteed level premium remains stable for the duration of the term, and the payout your beneficiary receives if you die during the coverage period is typically tax-free and has a steady value throughout the life of the policy.

A key step in purchasing a life insurance policy is choosing your life insurance beneficiary – the person (or entity) who will receive the cash benefit from your policy after you die. A beneficiary can be one, two, or more people; a trust you have set up with the proceeds administered by a trustee; a charity; or your estate.

When you designate beneficiaries, you have the final say over who receives your death benefit. If you do not choose one, your state's laws determine who gets it – and who wants to let their loved ones fend for themselves against a state bureaucracy? The primary beneficiary is first in line to receive your death benefit. If the primary beneficiary dies before you, a secondary or contingent beneficiary is the next in line. Some people also designate a final beneficiary in the event the primary and secondary beneficiaries die before they do. Some of the questions you will want to consider are:

- Who will need extra money when you pass away?
- Are there people who depend on you for financial support?
- Are there people who will bear certain expenses at your death?
- Who receives the proceeds if none of your beneficiaries survive you?
- Should the assets pass to your estate?
- Would the assets be better off in a trust?

With most policies, you can change your beneficiaries at any time. Review your policies regularly, and don't forget to make appropriate changes when your life changes, such as when you get married, have a baby, etcetera. You do not have to figure all this out by yourself. Contact your investment professional today to discuss your specific needs.

Universal life insurance provides permanent life insurance protection and access to tax-deferred cash values. Coverage continues for your entire life. No need to renew the policy with higher premiums. Some universal life policies can build cash value that you can access while you're alive. Because situations change, universal life insurance allows for some flexibility. As long as you remain within set boundaries, you can change the protection level of the policy and decide how frequently you pay your premium. As with most permanent life insurance, the death benefit paid to your beneficiaries is not subject to income taxes. Likewise, the cash value you withdraw from your policy to supplement your retirement is tax-free. A special combination of universal life insurance and long-term care coverage (sometimes called a hybrid life product) can provide cash value to help cover long-term care expenses. It also serves as a life insurance policy providing a death benefit to your beneficiaries. The major advantage of UL is flexibility. You can change the protection level of the policy and you control the amount of frequency of payments. This life insurance offers protection for your family and strategies for leaving a legacy to them. It can also help small business owners with continuation planning.

Variable universal life insurance is a permanent insurance policy that allows the ability to accumulate cash value while providing variety and control over professionally managed investment options. You have the freedom to monitor and make decisions on where to allocate your funds over time. This product also provides flexible premiums and flexible death benefits. It builds additional cash value that you can access, and earnings can grow income tax-free which allows them to accumulate faster.

Some of the disadvantages of life insurance include fixed periods of coverage. Most life insurance only covers individuals for a limited period. Many policies last for only one year or for five-year increments up to thirty years. However, options to renew the policies are often available. Old age or poor health can turn the flexibility of premiums into a disadvantage because premiums are known to increase substantially in cases when death becomes more likely. If you are older and in poor health, you will not obtain life insurance at reasonable premiums.

The advantages of life insurance are greater than its disadvantages; for instance, life insurance can be for many functions in estate planning including the following:

1. Term or whole life insurance can be purchased on an individual to provide funds for the surviving spouse or children when death occurs.
2. Whole life insurance can be purchased to provide income to the parents at retirement. This can occur by converting the policy to an annuity or by withdrawing the cash value.
3. Life insurance can provide dollars that can be passed as an inheritance to equalize your estate.
4. Life insurance can be used to provide funds for the payment of estate taxes, estate settlement costs, or debt obligations of the deceased.
5. Insurance can be purchased by the farming heir or heirs on their farming parents. It will provide income at the

time of the parent's death for the buyout of land, machinery, or operating assets from other heirs, if the parents have distributed their farm assets equally among all their children. A critical aspect in this example is that the farm or business heir owns the policy and makes all the premium payments. The farming parent or parents are the insured. The policy beneficiaries are the farm or business heirs. Using this format will ensure the death benefits go to the intended people.

6. Farming partners often buy insurance on each other. This process provides funds for buying out the deceased partner's assets if a premature death occurs. The result is that it enables the living partner to keep the farm or business intact.

7. Life insurance can be used to create or enhance an estate. It can be an estate building plan providing money to heirs.

8. There are some life insurance choices that enable people to draw on the death benefit to cover long-term healthcare costs. This can be beneficial for someone who may

not qualify for long-term care insurance
but would qualify for life insurance.

Ownership of the policy is sometimes treated lightly but is an important consideration, particularly in large estates. Generally, death benefits from life insurance are included in the estate of the owner of the policy, regardless of who is paying the insurance premium or who is named beneficiary. A change in ownership of a life insurance policy is a complex matter. One should review ownership provisions with an expert estate planner or insurance agent. Beneficiaries are the people who will get the death benefit proceeds of your life insurance. If your estate is the beneficiary of your life insurance, the plan established in your will or trust determines the distribution of death benefits.

A potential problem with this strategy is the insurance death benefit amount can increase the estate to a value above the applicable exclusion exemption amount for state and/or federal estate taxes. That causes an estate tax problem. This issue can be avoided if you place the life insurance in an irrevocable life insurance trust (ILIT). The trust owns the policy, but you are the insured. Because you do not own it, the death benefit is not included in your estate value, but you have the protection of the insurance. This is a complex area, so consult your attorney and insurance agent.

1. The entire amount of the benefit paid out to your beneficiaries or estate is included in your gross estate value for estate tax purposes if you are the owner of the policy. You could inadvertently create a taxable estate through purchasing life insurance if you do not realize the benefit amount will be included in your estate at death.
2. Life insurance proceeds paid to beneficiaries are not considered income to them for tax purposes.

An irrevocable life insurance trust (ILIT) can be of use in two ways. First, to avoid having to include the death benefit amount of a life insurance policy you own in your estate net worth, the insurance policy can be placed into an ILIT. The trust owns the policy and therefore the value is not included in your estate value. Second, if your business entity purchases life insurance for the owner/operators of the entity, the insurance can also be placed into an

ILIT. That prevents an individual who chooses to leave the entity from taking some of the insurance cash value with them. The ILIT preserves the insurance intact for those who remain in the entity. There are rules that need to be followed. The ILIT must be properly titled. The ILIT must have its own checking account and the address on the policy must be that of the trustee.

If you own a whole or universal life insurance policy purchased several years ago, it would be advisable to contact your insurance agent and request an in-force illustration to confirm the current value of your life insurance benefits. This process will help you assess how long the insurance policy will remain in force. Is it going to be available at your death or has the cash value declined to a point where the insurance lapses? This is a critical issue if the insurance was purchased a number of years ago and is a key part of your estate plan.

Life insurance plays a vital role in estate planning. It is important to coordinate all aspects of life insurance with your overall estate plan. Carefully analyze all factors before purchasing life insurance. Depending on family and circumstances, term life insurance might be more appropriate than whole life insurance and vice versa.

In conclusion, I strongly recommend for you to continue to evaluate your life insurance as family, estate, and business needs change throughout your lifetime. I have shared different ways in which business owners can create a family business legacy plan that is fair and equitable depending on their values, priorities, and family circumstances.

11

OBSTACLES WHEN CREATING AND IMPLEMENTING YOUR FAMILY BUSINESS LEGACY PLAN

"The greater the obstacle, the more glory in overcoming it."

— MOLIERE

In this chapter, we will talk about the obstacles that business owners face when creating and implementing a family business legacy plan. Often, a business owner will procrastinate and postpone creating a legacy plan without realizing what it will cost her and her family if she delays and does not to create and implement a family business legacy plan.

Creating and implementing a successful family business legacy plan is not easy; it is loaded with emotions. Therefore, it is highly recommended that the business owner takes time to work with her trusted advisors and family members to create and implement a successful family business legacy plan.

About 40 percent of the business owners I interviewed for this book did not yet have a succession plan because they did not know where to start and it is a time-consuming process. Also, some business owners felt it was too early to start a succession plan. It should be noted that it is never too early to plan for succession; therefore, I highly recommend that you start the conversation, especially if you are concerned about paying too much money on taxes which, if you properly plan, you can leave extra funds for your mission-based charities. You will also enjoy the comfort of knowing that your loved ones will be taken care of. Also, business succession requires the business owner to create a new vision for the company and a transfer plan that is fair and equitable to all parties involved, including outside talent and family members who are passionate about the business.

Remember, more time equals more options such as implementing tax strategies that may give you, your successor, and your business increased cash flow. Having more time also gives the business owner the opportunity to teach and train successors and to provide insightful information about the business. Business owners are often overwhelmed about succession planning, but you do not need to know all the answers. Hire qualified advisors to help you with the planning process.

Some business owners are concerned that they cannot find adequate advice. They do not know where do start. You can start by determining the value of your business based on earnings, book value, multiples of revenue, earnings before interest and taxes, and many other factors. Often, valuation is based on three major methods: the income approach, the cost approach, and the market or comparable sales approach. My preferred method of determining value is based on Earnings before Interest, Taxes, Depreciation, and Amortization (EBITDA). Business owners are often concerned about business succession planning because it is not just about naming your replacement. It involves comprehensive updates to every major facet of your operation including your foundational legal, financial, tax, and insurance systems.

In my experience as a family business advisor, the major obstacle for creating and implementing a family business legacy plan is that business owners believe that the process is too complex. With family businesses, succession planning is even more complicated because of the family members' relationships and high emotions involved and because many people do not feel comfortable discussing topics such as aging, death, and financial affairs. If transferring the business, it is important to realize that management and ownership are not the same. Based on the skillset, knowledge, and maturity of your children, you may or may not decide to transfer management of your business to just one of your children but transfer equal shares of ownership to all your children, whether they are actively involved in operating the business or not. However, it is critical to consult with your business advisors including your accountant, tax advisor, attorney, and family members to obtain advice about strategies to minimize taxes and create and implement a family business legacy plan that is fair and equitable to all stakeholders including the International Revenue Service (IRS).

Other business owners simply do not want to think about leaving the company yet. Some business owners believe that they are years away from stepping away from the business, and therefore, they do not need to worry about succession now. Some executives have immortality syndrome; they do not want to deal with their mortality. Also, for some executives, it is simply a matter of avoidance. They are not ready to give up their position in the company and cannot contemplate being replaced. Some business owners do not want to think about retirement because they have conflicts with family members or employees. Of the business owners who expect to retire or semi-retire within five years, 45 percent have not chosen a successor. Older business owners who are closer to retirement are no better at planning. Of the business owners sixty-one or older who are expected to retire within three years, 50 percent have not yet chosen a successor, and those who do often try to clone themselves. Choosing a successor is not about cloning yourself. It is about finding someone to build upon what you have accomplished and take your business to the next level. The most qualified successor may turn out to be someone whose leadership style, skills, and business strategies are quite different from yours. Provided the two of you share the same fundamental values and vision for the company, you must not let the fact they approach things in a different way than you cloud your judgment.

One of the major obstacles to create and implement a family business legacy plan is the lack of knowledge of estate taxes. Estate tax is a tax levied on the net value of the estate of a deceased person before distribution to the heirs. It consists of an accounting of everything you own or have certain interests in on the date of your death. The fair market value of these items is used, not what you paid for them. The includible property may consist of cash and securities, real estate, insurance, trusts, annuities, business interests, and other assets.

Often high-net-worth individuals and business owners are concerned about the cost of estate taxes. According to the current Internal Revenue Service guidelines, estates of decedent residents' citizens of the United States; the simple estates including cash, publicly traded securities, small amounts of other easily valued assets, and no special deductions or elections; or jointly held property do not require the filing of an estate tax return.

At the time of this writing, a filing is required for estates with combined gross assets and prior taxable gifts exceeding $11,580,000 in 2020 and $11,700,000 in 2021. For estates of non- citizens of the United States, the estate tax is a tax on the transfer of U.S.-situated property, which may include both tangible and intangible assets owned at the decedent's date of death. The computation of the tax requires that you state the total value of assets situated in the United States and generally requires a separate statement of the total value of assets situated outside the United States. The two totals are the "gross estate in the United States" and the "gross estate outside the United States." Property includible in these two totals may consist of cash and securities, real estate, insurance, trusts, annuities, business interests, and other assets.

To value the assets held at the date of death, the fair market value is used, not necessarily what was paid for them or what their values were when they were acquired. If you do not file your taxes on a timely basis and/or you have a past-due tax return, you will have to pay to the Internal Revenue Service (IRS) interest charges and late payment penalties. Also, the IRS can impose a federal tax lien which is the government's legal claim against your property when you neglect or fail to pay a tax debt. The lien protects the government's interest in all your property, including real estate, personal property, and financial assets. The IRS may also file a public document, the Notice of Federal Tax Lien, to alert creditors that the government has a legal right to your property.

The cost of not creating a well-established and codified formal plan for succession may produce disastrous consequences for a family business. As we can see, postponing the creation and implementation of a tax effective family business legacy plan can be an expensive and annoying experience. Therefore, I encourage you to stop procrastinating and start the conversation today with your trusted advisors to provide guidance and clarity to enable you to create a family business legacy plan that works for your personal, business, and family needs.

CONCLUSION – HOW DOES IT FEEL TO CREATE A FAIR AND EQUITABLE FAMILY BUSINESS LEGACY PLAN?

"Success is not measured by money or power or social rank. Success is measured by your discipline and inner peace."

— MIKE DITKA

In this final chapter, my goal is for you to feel happy that you have created and implemented a family business legacy plan to secure the continuity of your business and for you to enjoy peace and harmony with your family.

From the beginning of this book, I wrote about your need to create a family business legacy plan to legally avoid paying too much money in taxes and to give you peace of mind. Therefore, throughout the book, I shared ideas to minimize taxes and to create and implement a plan that is fair, equitable, and in alignment with your values. I hope that after reading this book, you too will know how to create a family business legacy plan and you feel excited about it because you now have a clear vision about your plan and you are no longer worried about losing money to irresponsible choices due to lack of proper business and estate planning.

You will face challenges and opportunities as you proceed to create and implement your unique plan, and I know that you have the fortitude to overcome those challenges and take advantages of the opportunities. I hope that you will take time to read and implement some of the ideas identified in this book. You must decide whether you want business continuity or to sell your business; whichever path you choose, it will be the right decision for you! However, you must surround yourself with the right advisors such as your tax accountant, attorney, business advisor, etcetera to help you create and implement this life changing decision.

Like Stephanie, the owner of an import-export business owner I introduced to you in Chapter 1, you do not need to have all your family business legacy issues figured out to start the process, but you do need the right attitude and frame of mind to decide that enough is enough and start the process of creating a family business legacy plan to enable you to identify and prioritize your personal and business assets; to help you minimize federal, state, and city taxes; and maximize the money that you will keep for yourself, your family, and for your charitable organizations. The biggest mistake successful business owners make is not to seek professional advice and instead worry about losing money due to irresponsible choices.

You do not need to have all your family business legacy issues figured out to start the process. The family business legacy plan process will enable you to identify and prioritize your personal and business assets; will minimize federal, state, and city taxes; and enable you to keep more money for your family and for your charitable organizations. The biggest mistake successful business owners make is not to seek professional advice and instead worry about losing money due to irresponsible choices.

In Stephanie's case, it only took weeks to understand her overall business and prioritize her primary goals and objectives which enabled us to help her create a financial forecast to determine the potential value of the business. We were also able to identify the most important issues facing her business and create a fair and equitable family business succession plan that allowed the company to grow and diversify while identifying currency hedging strategies such as foreign exchange forward contracts to better manage the Argentinian currency fluctuation.

When creating your family business legacy plan, identify your goals and objectives and decide on a timeframe to accomplish the desired outcome. It is important to identify the family members who will contribute to the creation of the legacy plan, your negotiable versus non-negotiable considerations, and even those who may not be happy with your decision.

Some of my clients have found out the importance of creating and implementing charter provisions that promote family unity and affiliation. The charter provisions capture important benefits, both tangible and intangible to facilitate a smooth process for leadership succession – a tangible benefit. Each generation will find their passion, and each family member must earn their place within the organization, be properly trained, and compensated accordingly.

It is important to identify a complete inventory of your personal assets and your business balance sheet and to seek advice from your advisors and family members to get clear on your short- and long-term goals. Envision what your ideal family business legacy plan will look like, what it will accomplish.

Create a value mission and vision statement with your family members' participation; these values will become your family's north star when your family is facing challenging business and financial decisions.

In a business, a balance sheet is a specific financial document that summarizes your business assets. It is a record that objectively determines your company's value based on its assets, liabilities, and shareholder's equity. When we take a family enterprise view, we "begin with an end in mind," and rather than looking at three to five years, family businesses often plan longer term. For instance, a 100-year business legacy plan covers three generations, which is far more to consider from a planning perspective.

A family enterprise is composed of personal, work, and business. The goal is to increase the value of the family assets over time, to decrease threatening liabilities, and to increase the family enterprise equity overall. Some of the ways that families define wealth include financial, structural, heritage and values, community, human talent, and family. Combined, these represent the total value of the family enterprise and include much more than just the bank account balance. They consider individual and family success, preservation, happiness, and intellectual wealth. These are truly the foundations of a successful family enterprise.

The time to act is now. If you are still reading this book, I know that you ready to start a family business legacy plan to protect, preserve your financial wellbeing, to live the lifestyle you always dreamed of, and to avail yourself with life choices leading to total fulfillment and happiness. I wish you much success in creating and implementing a fair and equitable family business legacy plan.

In closing, my wish for you is that you feel happy that you have created and implemented a family business legacy plan to secure the continuity of your business and enjoy peace and harmony with your family.

I was inspired to write this book because creating and implementing a family business legacy plan is not easy, and it is loaded with emotions about being equitable and fair to family members and stakeholders.

I would like to thank my growing family! Stephen, my husband for over forty years, and our sons Michael and Tommy and their families, who are my biggest fans – always have been and always will be. I love and appreciate them deeply! My brothers Francisco, Sergio, Ruben, and Eloy and my sister Zulema are my proudest fans – seeing them beam with pride over my accomplishments and having their encouraging thoughts mean a lot to me. Thank you for your patience and for your unconditional love. Thank you for your sense of humor, your gentleness, and acceptance. May our family legacy make us proud!

Also, special thanks to my Harvard Business School/OPM32 friends, The Old Guard – my gratefulness for our more than twenty years of friendship as OPMers colleagues and friends has no bounds. We were a powerhouse team then and we are a powerhouse team today. We are a team for life! So much love and appreciation for you all. Thank you!

Maria L. Ellis, MBA is a best-selling author of *Achieve Financial Freedom*, a roadmap to financial success. She is graduate of the Harvard Business School Owner-President Management Program and earned her bachelor's degree in business administration as well as her MBA from the University of Massachusetts in Amherst. As a former international banker, investments and real estate advisor, Maria has specialized in converting clients' financial objectives into successful action plans. Maria has both the know-how and the market contacts having worked at Bank of America, Citibank, the MONY Group, Northwestern Mutual, Citi Habitats, and Keller Williams New York City and Keller Williams Palm Beaches.

Maria's background includes board and leadership positions at the College of Mount Saint Vincent, the American Association of University Women, Harvard Club, New York City, Virginia Gildersleeve International Fund, and The Empire State New York City, AAUW. Maria is also a pro-bono consultant at the Harvard Business School Club of New York City Community Partners and applies her business skills to a variety of topics including strategic planning, marketing, finance, governance, and organizational development.

Difference Press is the exclusive publishing arm of The Author Incubator, an educational company for entrepreneurs – including life coaches, healers, consultants, and community leaders – looking for a comprehensive solution to get their books written, published, and promoted. Its founder, Dr. Angela Lauria, has been bringing to life the literary ventures of hundreds of authors-in-transformation since 1994.

A boutique-style self-publishing service for clients of The Author Incubator, Difference Press boasts a fair and easy-to-understand profit structure, low-priced author copies, and author-friendly contract terms. Most importantly, all of our #incubatedauthors maintain ownership of their copyright at all times.

LET'S START A MOVEMENT WITH YOUR MESSAGE

In a market where hundreds of thousands of books are published every year and are never heard from again, The Author Incubator is different. Not only do all Difference Press books reach Amazon best-seller status, but all of our authors are actively changing lives and making a difference.

Since launching in 2013, we've served over 500 authors who came to us with an idea for a book and were able to write it and get it self-published in less than six months. In addition, more than 100 of those books were picked up by traditional publishers and are now available in bookstores. We do this by selecting the highest quality and highest potential applicants for our future programs.

Our program doesn't only teach you how to write a book – our team of coaches, developmental editors, copy editors, art directors, and marketing experts incubate you from having a book idea to being a published, best-selling author, ensuring that the book you create can actually make a difference in the world. Then we give you the training you need to use your book to make the difference in the world, or to create a business out of serving your readers.

ARE YOU READY TO MAKE A DIFFERENCE?

You've seen other people make a difference with a book. Now it's your turn. If you are ready to stop watching and start taking massive action, go to http://theauthorincubator.com/apply/.

"Yes, I'm ready!"

Thank you for reading my family business legacy book which I wrote with you in mind. It is my earnest desire that you know the importance of creating a family business legacy plan that is fair and equitable to enable you to have peace of mind and to live and enjoy your life along with family, friends, and significant others. Therefore, I am offering you a complimentary consultation and a free copy of this book by subscribing to https://financiallegacy.live/